MID-CONTINENT PUBLIC LIBRARY - BTM

3 0003 01244959 9

D1470553

WITHDRAWN
FROM THE RECORDS OF THE
MID-CONTINENT PUBLIC LIBRARY

Mid-Continent Public Library
15616 East US Highway 24
Independence, MO 64050

African Elephants

by Kari Schuetz

BELLWETHER MEDIA • MINNEAPOLIS, MN

Note to Librarians, Teachers, and Parents:

Blastoff! Readers are carefully developed by literacy experts and combine standards-based content with developmentally appropriate text.

Level 1 provides the most support through repetition of high-frequency words, light text, predictable sentence patterns, and strong visual support.

Level 2 offers early readers a bit more challenge through varied simple sentences, increased text load, and less repetition of high-frequency words.

Level 3 advances early-fluent readers toward fluency through increased text and concept load, less reliance on visuals, longer sentences, and more literary language.

Level 4 builds reading stamina by providing more text per page, increased use of punctuation, greater variation in sentence patterns, and increasingly challenging vocabulary.

Level 5 encourages children to move from "learning to read" to "reading to learn" by providing even more text, varied writing styles, and less familiar topics.

Whichever book is right for your reader, Blastoff! Readers are the perfect books to build confidence and encourage a love of reading that will last a lifetime!

This edition first published in 2012 by Bellwether Media, Inc.

No part of this publication may be reproduced in whole or in part without written permission of the publisher. For information regarding permission, write to Bellwether Media, Inc., Attention: Permissions Department, 5357 Penn Avenue South, Minneapolis, MN 55419.

Library of Congress Cataloging-in-Publication Data

Schuetz, Kari.
  African elephants / by Kari Schuetz.
      p. cm. – (Blastoff! Readers. Animal safari)
  Includes bibliographical references and index.
  Summary: "Developed by literacy experts for students in kindergarten through grade three, this book introduces African elephants to young readers through leveled text and related photos"–Provided by publisher.
  ISBN 978-1-60014-600-8 (hardcover : alk. paper)
  1. African elephant–Juvenile literature. I. Title.
  QL737.P98S394 2012
  599.67'4–dc22   2011008181

Text copyright © 2012 by Bellwether Media, Inc. BLASTOFF! READERS and associated logos are trademarks and/or registered trademarks of Bellwether Media, Inc. SCHOLASTIC, CHILDREN'S PRESS, and associated logos are trademarks and/or registered trademarks of Scholastic Inc.

Printed in the United States of America, North Mankato, MN.

080111   1187

Contents

What Are African Elephants?

African elephants are the largest land animals on Earth.

They have long **trunks**. They can pinch with the ends of their trunks.

Eating

African elephants use their trunks to grab plants, fruits, and other food.

They use strong **tusks** to dig up roots. Tusks also help them strip bark from trees.

Staying Cool

African elephants
must stay cool
in hot weather.
They spray water
on their bodies.

They also cover their bodies with dust. The dust helps block the sun.

Herds

African elephants
travel in **herds**.
They roam forests
and **savannahs**.

African elephants **trumpet** to warn the herd of danger.

They often twist
their trunks together
to say hello.
Elephant hug!

Glossary

herds—groups of elephants that live and travel together

savannahs—grasslands with very few trees

trumpet—to push air through the trunk to make a horn sound

trunks—the long noses and upper lips of elephants

tusks—large, long teeth that stick out of the mouths of some animals

To Learn More

AT THE LIBRARY

Buttar, Debbie. *Tonga: The African Elephant Story*. London, U.K.: GMEC Publishing, 2008.

Doudna, Kelly. *It's a Baby African Elephant!* South Pasadena, Calif.: SandCastle, 2008.

Meltzer Kleinhenz, Sydnie. *Elephants*. Mankato, Minn.: Capstone Press, 2008.

ON THE WEB

Learning more about African elephants is as easy as 1, 2, 3.

1. Go to www.factsurfer.com.

2. Enter "African elephants" into the search box.

3. Click the "Surf" button and you will see a list of related Web sites.

With factsurfer.com, finding more information is just a click away.

Index

The images in this book are reproduced through the courtesy of: Four Oaks, front cover, p. 7; Jürgen + Christine Sohns / Photolibrary, p. 5; Digfoto Digfoto / Photolibrary, p. 7 (small); Martin B Withers / FLPA / Minden Pictures, pp. 9 (top), 15; Adriaan Venter, p. 9 (left); Henry Wilson, p. 9 (right); Manoj Shah / Getty Images, p. 11; Chris Gomersall / Alamy, p. 13; Martin Harvey / Kimballstock, p. 17; Peter Malsbury / Getty Images, p. 19; Ferrero-Labat / ardea.com, p. 21.